Life After You

What Your Death From Drugs Leaves Behind

LINDA LAJTERMAN

ISBN: 0692260889
ISBN 13: 9780692260883
Library of Congress Control Number: 2014951780
WAT-AGE Publishing, Alexandria, VA (PI)

No farewell words were spoken,
no time to say goodbye.
You were gone before we knew it,
and only God knows why.

Author unknown

Dedication

This book is dedicated to every mother, father, brother, and sister who has lost a precious family member to drugs. We include the grandmothers, grandfathers, aunts, uncles, and cousins in this dedication as well as girlfriends, boyfriends, husbands and wives.

From our family to yours,
we understand your pain,
we understand your loss.

Tito, Linda, Michael, Andrea, Alex and Colleen

Table of Contents

One

A LETTER TO PARENTS

Mourning the loss of my precious son, Danny, writing has become a therapeutic activity. Words, however, often seem inadequate to describe how his death has affected our family and changed our lives forever. Devastated to have lost my baby, my youngest child, I hope that writing about my family's experience will help kids understand what they do to themselves and to their families when they use drugs. Even if only a small percentage of readers are touched by what I have to say, this book will be worth the effort.

I'm addressing this letter to you, the parent, and the other adults in a young person's life - older siblings, relatives, teachers, physicians, drug counselors, and others - with the hope that you will place this book into the hands of a young adolescent, teen, or young adult who needs to confront the cold, hard facts of drug abuse. This book is not a summary of the various drugs young people use. I'm not going to list them or their side effects. What I am going to do is shock teenagers into understanding what happens when that brief high ends in lasting death. Be warned: it's not a pretty picture. But if all those drug prevention classes or even trips to rehab have not kept your teen away from dangerous substances, this book may be your only hope.

The effects of Danny's death have rippled through the lives of everyone who knew him. That could be a book by itself! I do not wish to see another loving family suffer this pain and I don't want to see another young person die from using drugs. I do not want to see another teen spend his or her life struggling with addiction. I do not want to see another parent worried that a son or daughter may be the next one to die. I want to scream at every kid in the world - STOP THIS NOW! Think about what you are doing! Why would you do this? I can't do that, but through my words - a graphic description of death and the guilt and shame that follow addiction - I hope to present a far different perspective on drug use, one that is never presented in schools.

Bad Choices, Bad Results

My son had no idea that his poor choices would cost him his life and devastate his family. Most teens who experiment with drugs don't either. They think it will never happen to them. My son didn't know the fatal drug he used was concocted by a drug dealer who was an evil, greedy, monster, someone who cut and mixed drugs without any knowledge of dosage proportion. A monster posing as a friend to the local teenagers, selling them whatever drug they requested. This monster doesn't resemble the drug dealers often depicted in TV dramas. Rather, he's the father of three children and lives in the next town. Two of his kids went to high school with my son. There was no need to travel to the inner city; drugs were plentiful and right around the corner, being supplied by a trusted dad in the community. The order was filled through the use of a phone app, the record of the sale ultimately erased. There are monsters like this all over the world and they are not going away as long as there are customers buying their drugs. Drug dealers are everywhere - in schools, college dorms, hair salons, and any other place you can imagine. These drug dealers look normal and non threatening. Your teens need to understand that these people and the drugs they sell are dangerous and, in many cases, lethal.

Raising awareness about drug abuse is now my personal campaign. This role is not one I ever wanted or sought. But my experience has opened my eyes. We don't see enough warnings to teens about where the drugs are coming from and who is mixing them. Law enforcement officials focus on arresting drug dealers and confiscating their supplies. But as long as there's a demand for the drugs, there will always be someone ready to be the supplier. We need to diminish the demand so the supply can sit and rot.

After the death of my son, I posted a letter on Facebook meant to warn the local families who like us thought: "Drugs and my kid? Never!" We learned our lesson the hard way, that as much as a parent knows about a son or daughter, many teens still have a secret life, one they become skilled at hiding from their families. My letter went viral and I have heard from families all over the world who are dealing with kids who are addicted, in and out of rehab, and dying. Young mothers wrote to me scared out of their minds for their young children. What will the world be like for them? Addicts wrote to me pouring out their stories and validating what my letter stated. The problem of drug use is beyond any local police department or county drug enforcement agency's ability. It is a worldwide problem that does not appear to be going away anytime soon.

I had a conversation with the principal of our local high school after Danny's death. We discussed how it took years to address bullying and it may take years to address this present epidemic of drug use with a combined home, community, and school effort. In the meantime, while the school systems are doing what they can with the educational tools available, these tactics obviously are not working.

Young people buy into the fallacy that doing drugs is fun and that nothing bad will happen to them. One tip off: if your child's friends are experimenting with drugs, chances are your teen is, too. Whether you suspect your teen is using or not, start the conversation. Explain the risks involved. Talk about the greedy drug dealers who will cut and mix drugs with poison to increase profits. Your child may be afraid to admit he or she tried any type of substance. Often a young person, frightened by drug use that is out of control, will be reluctant to ask for help. Express your unconditional love and your willingness to do whatever you can for your teen under any circumstance. I didn't get that chance with my son. Don't let that happen to your child.

At the end of this book, I will give teens some advice on how to ask their parents for help. I also include ways a teen can help a friend who seems to be on a downward spiral. If you are lucky enough to have your child tell you about his or her drug use, take action. Don't wait. If another parent or one of your child's friends warns you about your child using drugs, don't fall back into the "not my kid" mindset. Please remember what happened to us! I wish someone had taken a risk and come to us with the information. We would have listened. We did not know what Danny was doing. He hid his drug use very well. I have heard this story from countless families around the world. Many drug users like my son are able to function perfectly well without anyone - even family members - suspecting drug use. I would not have known what Danny was doing unless he or someone else told me or unless he got arrested. Do not kill the messenger who is trying to save your child from death. Your family is lucky if someone cares enough to step out of their comfort zone and tell you. Thank them, don't get angry at them. You will be very angry if your child dies and you found out that they knew and did nothing to help. Trust me on that one!

I am a nurse, but not an expert on drugs or addiction. I am, unfortunately, an expert on what my son's death from drugs has done to my family. I know that kids don't understand what can happen to them, even from just one time using drugs. Many of them fail to grasp the finality of death. They have no idea that using drugs to fit in will leave behind their devastated families, the people who love them the most.

Parents, make your teens read this book, and then ask them to read it again. Tell them you love them every single day. Don't let your child become another statistic.

Linda Lajterman

Two

PREFACE

On February 23, 2014, after continuous pounding on the door of my son's bedroom without a response, we broke it down. At first glance the room looked empty. I was relieved, reassuring myself with: "He isn't even home!" Then a scream from my husband snapped me back into reality. My son was in the room, in his desk chair, slumped sideways toward the floor. My husband pulled Danny out of the seat and placed him on his back. His father, girlfriend, and I all screamed simultaneously. My son's face was completely distorted. It was swollen, dark blue, and unrecognizable. I was in shock but my instincts as a nurse kicked in and I tried to feel for a pulse. Unable to find one, I quickly called 911. I don't remember what I said to the 911 operator, but I did make sure to give our address.

The screams coming from our house were heard by all of our neighbors who quickly gathered outside to see what had happened. We were going crazy. We were panicking. I called our older children to tell them to come to our home immediately. I don't remember doing so, but I blurted out, "we think Danny is dead!" This left them to drive to the house in a dangerous frenzy. For that, I am eternally sorry, but I was in shock.

The sirens wailed as police cars and the ambulance came down our street. The police went into Danny's room, took a look at him, and quickly escorted us away. They led us into the kitchen while an officer stood guard in front of the area where his bedroom was located to keep us out. We were told he was gone and were not allowed near him again. That was the last time we saw our son. We never had a chance to kiss him goodbye.

After pleading with the officers for information, they said they found drugs in his room and on his desk. We were all in total shock. We had no clue Danny was using any drugs, and now he was dead.

A full investigation was begun to determine what he took, whom he was with, where the drugs came from, and what else was in his room. The local police and county drug enforcement agency officers were in and out of our house, but mostly in his room searching every inch of his space.

They went through each and every one of his belongings, taking his cell phone and laptop away for a more thorough investigation. Every text message, email, and photo would be scrutinized and used for evidence against the drug dealer. They would also be logging into his Facebook and Twitter accounts. In the meantime, our house quickly filled up with family, friends, and neighbors.

It took over eight hours before they finished searching his room and collecting all of the evidence. The coroner's van came to our house to bring our dead son to the county medical examiner's office. The news of Danny's death spread like wildfire through our small community. People who hadn't been to our house in years, suddenly showed up. They didn't belong with us at this time, but they showed up anyway. Maybe to be nosy, maybe to be supportive? Who knows why? The house was full. We were in shock and clueless about what to do next.

The memory of the remainder of that night, along with the next few days remains a blur. However, the sight of our son's face and lifeless body is so embedded in our minds, we cannot close our eyes without that vision coming through. Hopefully those memories will recede with time and we will be able to remember our handsome, funny, and wonderful son. A young man who was loved by everyone who knew him.

Our Typical Son

Danny was a typical 19 year old. He attended college, got decent grades, had a girlfriend, and lots of friends. He enjoyed video games, watched TV shows and movies. He spent a lot of time at home with his girlfriend, just hanging out. He was friends with everyone. He was nice to each person he met and made an effort to make any and every kid he met feel like an important human being. Danny had an older brother and sister who adored him. He played jokes on his siblings, called them all the time, sent texts with funny messages and made time to hang out with them. He had grandmothers and lots of cousins, aunts, and uncles and went to all the family parties. He loved the holidays and loved his family. He ate breakfast at the kitchen counter and would still watch cartoons. He ate dinner with us almost every night. He called us when he was out just to check in. He had hobbies and interests. He had plans for his future. Danny told us he loved us every day and always greeted us with a smile and a hug. Like most teenagers, he also had a secret life when he was with his friends. A part of his life he hid very well from his family and many others. He would look us in the eye and tell us he would never try any type of drug. He would tell us he knew all about the dangers of using drugs and that he knew many kids who were "out of control." He didn't know his bad choices would take his life. **He did not want to die. Danny was probably very much like you!**

This book is written by a mother who lost her son. His father, brother, sister, girlfriend and I are shattered, broken, and will <u>never</u> be the same. What I have written also reflects a family who lost a future brother in law, a grandson, nephew, and cousin to drugs. Our pain is tremendous and permanent. We can only hope that with each day our hurt becomes more tolerable.

I am writing these words less than two months after Danny's death. But this book is not for him; it's for you. It's too late for me to help my son, but not too late for me to help other teens who are using or thinking of using drugs. I hope to wake you up and make you think twice when confronted with decisions that may prove deadly. When you use drugs you can die, and your death will change the lives of your family and loved ones forever.

I know you receive many forms of drug awareness education, but based on the recent statistics of addiction, overdose, and drug related deaths in the past few years, the message is definitely not getting across. I have personally read the experiences of over a thousand families from all over the world. They shared what this terrible epidemic of drug addiction has done to their lives, and I know we are not alone in our grief and sorrow. The pain this causes your family is immeasurable.

Three

INTRODUCTION

You don't think this will ever happen to you. It happens to "other kids." I am sure you think nothing bad will ever happen to you, your brain, or your heart. That only happens in the boring stuff they make you read in health class. Today is the day you <u>will</u> think about it as if it has happened to you:

You died from using drugs.

What you swallowed, snorted, injected or smoked may have been laced with some type of poison, or you may have taken too much. It started because you thought it was fun to get high, and now you are dead.

I will walk you through this experience. I will show you how the choice you made to experiment with drugs can kill you and how that affects the very people who love you the most. Whether you are trying to fit in, having trouble coping, or are just an edgy type of person who is searching for thrills, **you can die**.

I will show you what happens to your body. It will not be fun and it definitely is not what you will expect. I am not going to color this to protect your feelings. I am not going to shield you from the reality of what will happen. This is the absolute truth.

Read this, re-read it and re-read it again and try to imagine it was **YOU** who died. This is what you will go through, and what you left your loved ones behind to experience. Then, I want you to go back to the very first time you thought it was fun or you tried to fit in with a bunch of your friends and see if it was worth it.

Four

THE MESSAGE

This book is not to educate you about the science of what an opiate or any type of hallucinogenic drug does to your brain and body. You had all that in school and didn't listen or care because it didn't stop you.

You didn't learn the lesson that when you use drugs, the drugs are in control, not you.

Reality Check. Death is forever. Death is eternal darkness. There are no second chances; you don't wake up three hours later. There are no do-overs. You are gone!!

You do not want to die before your life even starts. You do not want to cause excruciating pain to the people you love. Is getting high so great that you would risk your life? Are you willing to die to fit in with your friends? You came into this world loved and adored by your family. They care about you more than anyone else. Do you want to cause your family to suffer just so you can fit in with the "popular" crowd?

Maybe this book will stop you from trying drugs. It may help you stay strong through rehab and healing. It just may scare the daylights out of you to stop the experimenting before you become an addict. Or it may make you **think of what can happen** if you start to relapse. Only you have the power to help yourself.

If you are an addict who is not getting help, you probably won't care about this message, but someday you may. Keep this book around and read it when you are ready to help yourself. There may be a moment when you realize what your drug use can do to you and your family. You may actually start to care.

Five

YOUR DEATH

*M*ost of you have never seen a dead person anywhere other than at a funeral where the body is dressed nicely, the hair is styled, and the corpse is resting comfortably in a soft pillow-looking casket. When you die, it is nothing like what you see on television or in movies, and <u>definitely</u> not like a funeral. You will not be peacefully lying with your eyes closed looking like you are sleeping. You will not look like yourself at all.

Depending on how long it takes for someone to find you, your blood will pool in different areas of your body causing you to become different shades of red, blue and black. Your body will be ice cold. Your face will be enlarged and discolored. It will look as though you have something in your mouth, but guess what? It's your tongue, and it's swollen and protruding. Your eyes may be half open or all the way open. Your arms and hands can be dark blue, almost black. If you were dead for a few hours before you were found, you will have rigor mortis. Your face, arms, legs, head and neck will be stiff and in the position you were in when you took your last breath. You will look very scary.

If you want to know what happens to your body during death, there are plenty of places on the Internet where you can learn the scientific process of cellular death and the stages your body will go through during the first hours. You may not find this out unless you really research. When you die, extremely embarrassing things will happen to you. The contents of your bowels and bladder are emptied out. You will be soaked with urine and stool. It may be in front of your friends if they stayed around to watch you die, but probably not. They most likely ran out on you once they saw you were in trouble. They left you to die alone because they were scared of getting caught. I have heard from many families that their teen was left by their "friends" to die alone. Hopefully they called for help, but you never know what damage to your brain and organs will happen if you are saved. We will talk about that in another section.

If you are found at home, you have now caused your family to experience one of the worst shocks of their lives. This will be the vision your mother, father, brother or sister goes to sleep with, wakes up to and sees throughout the day for months to come. They will have flashbacks of this vision, trouble sleeping, memory loss, depression and enormous amounts of anger and guilt for a long time. Whoever found you may need psychiatric care or medications to deal with this daily vision. Your family may have trouble remembering for a long time your face any other way than how you looked on the day you died. Every time they close their eyes, your dead face and body is what they will see.

Please don't forget that after you die, the police will go through each and every one of your belongings in your room and in your car. As they did to Danny's, your cell phone and your computer will be taken for investigation. They will go through your Facebook, Twitter, Instagram or any other social media account. They will read all your text messages, look at all your pictures, read your school notebooks or your diary. If you continue to use drugs, keep in mind that your private life will be open to everyone and you can do nothing about it.

If you are not at your house, whoever does find you will not care as much. You're just another kid who has died from drugs. You're just another dead body. They will sleep without any problems. You have become one of the growing statistics of drug related deaths because you thought it was fun to get high.

Everyone does die eventually, but hopefully after having a chance for a long productive life full of fun experiences. An older person dying is a natural part of life. People with terminal illnesses have been sick for a long time. You should not die at an age where you haven't even had the chance to do anything but get high with your so-called "friends." We will discuss them later.

Before your dead body is removed from wherever they found you, the medical examiner's office will request permission from your family to perform an autopsy. Your parents or next of kin, now in shock, will have to sign the consent. They will all look at each other waiting for someone to make that decision, and one of them will have to sign the form. In many states, any suspicious or unattended death will require an autopsy automatically so your family may not have a choice.

An autopsy is needed to find out what caused your death. During the autopsy, you will lie on a table in the county medical examiner's office and your body will be cut open for testing of your tissues, organs, and blood. You will be placed on a large rubber block to raise your upper body. The coroner will cut you open with a "Y" incision, laying your torso wide open. He removes and dissects your chest, abdominal and pelvic organs, and (if necessary) your brain. The officials need to see what was in your body that caused your death, and if there was any other reason you died. You are dead and won't feel it, but your family will have to envision your body being cut open while you lie alone on a cold table. They are not permitted to be there with you. This is another traumatic image they will have to try to get out of their minds for months to come.

After they cut you up and put you back together, you will go into cold storage. You will remain there until you are taken to the funeral home or crematorium. Your family will not get the results back from the medical examiner's office for at least eight weeks. But don't worry; your family will get a verbal report if they find a cause of death other than drugs.

By this time, the shock of your death will cause many of your family members to get sick. It is not uncommon for your mother and/or father to experience chest pain and shortness of breath. Their blood pressure will go haywire and they may require tranquilizers and sleeping pills. They may be rushed to the hospital themselves. (The ambulance made two trips to my house for me alone!) They will not be able to sleep or eat for days. They will have nightmares. Shock and stress are very powerful and harmful to the body. Your death has probably now taken a few years off your family's lives as well.

At this time, your family will still be in shock and the reality that you are never coming home has not quite set in. They will probably try to make believe you are at school or out somewhere, that you are not gone forever. But you **are** gone forever.

Over the next day or so, friends and family members will be sending food, plants and assorted baskets to your house. Your family will be overwhelmed by the graciousness of people who feel badly for them about their dead child.

Six

YOUR FUNERAL

Within a day or so after your death, your family now has the job of planning your funeral. Should they bury you in a cemetery or have you cremated? If you are buried, they have to pick out and buy a casket and buy a plot in a cemetery or a mausoleum. They will have to pick out flowers to be placed around your coffin. They will have to pick out a card that visitors will take home with them, a card that will be printed with your name, the date of your birth and death along with a quote, often a religious one. If you are cremated, they need to choose an urn or container for your ashes. Your parents, brothers, sisters, and family will have a meeting to plan what they will do with your body and choose the type of memorial services.

Someone has to write your obituary and spread the news of your funeral. Hopefully, you will have someone available to do that for your family; they won't be in any shape for writing at this time. Maybe you should have that ready for them now if you plan to continue experimenting and using drugs. Thank goodness Facebook and Twitter are good ways to spread the news. Make sure someone in your family is friends with you online so your pals can write on your wall, tweet about you and know when to come to your funeral. Chances are, your cool friends won't be reading the obituary section of the newspaper.

In case you are wondering, most parents don't have a funeral plan in place for their children. You have now added extra pain for your family to deal with because of your death from using drugs. They probably are still in shock, crying on and off all day long, can't sleep and can't make decisions. They will need help from other family members or friends. Either your older siblings or a relative may have to fill in for your parents and/or hold their hands through this process. If it is one of your siblings, you have now caused them to experience planning a funeral for a brother or sister, and having to be strong for the whole family.

Everyone will break down several times during the planning. Parents are not supposed to bury their child. Siblings are not supposed to plan funerals for each other. Think about how you would feel and what you would do if you were the one to have to make the funeral plans for your brother or sister.

Are you proud of yourself? There is more so get ready. This is just the basics of what happened to you, and what you did to your family because you wanted to fit in. You followed the crowd. You were a follower, not a leader.

On a more practical note, you may have stolen and sold anything of value that your family had for drug money. Now they have to figure out how to come up with the money to pay for your funeral. If they don't have a large sum of money in the bank, they will have to borrow the money from someone, use a credit card, or ask for donations. If they can't come up with the money, an option would be for them not to claim your body, leave you at the medical examiner's office, and you will be cremated at the state expense. They won't get your ashes. Your family may have to hold your memorial service in a park or at their home.

We come from the New York metropolitan area. At this time, a funeral can run anywhere from $6,000 and up depending on what they do with your body. To bury you in a cemetery can cost another $15,000 and up if they have to buy a place to put you.

So simply stated, your using drugs has:

- Cost you your life.
- Devastated your family.
- Caused them financial distress (if they are not already there from trying to pay for your stay or multiple stays in rehab).

If you don't plan to stop experimenting with drugs or will relapse after rehab, please don't sell everything your family has worked for since they will need money to bury you.

Does experimenting with drugs still sound fun?

One more thing, please make sure you have a nice suit or dress available to be buried in; your family won't be in any shape to go shopping to pick out your funeral outfit. Your mom will choose what you will spend eternity in from your closet. You probably won't like it.

It is important for you to know that your elderly relatives will be very embarrassed to tell their friends you died from drugs. They may make up a story about your heart stopping or a disease you didn't have. They didn't grow up in an era where any type of recreational substance use was remotely acceptable, and this is the only way they can cope with this humiliation. Don't be surprised if most of your relatives are embarrassed that you died from drugs. Your close family knows how wonderful you were. Other people will only see you as DRUGS. Grandma and grandpa will probably not want to face anyone again. Your drug use brought shame to your family. I hope you're getting prouder and prouder of yourself.

Depending on your family preferences, religion or customs, the day of your funeral will eventually arrive. Your family will be numb as they dress to go to the funeral of the teenager they loved so much. They may feel like this is an out of body experience and be in disbelief that they are going to the funeral of their child. This day will eventually be a blur to your family afterword.

The immediate family goes in to see you first before your coffin is open to the public. Your mother, father, brothers, and sisters will be overcome with emotions through this funeral process. They may scream, they may faint, and everyone will be crying. It is highly possible they will need medication to get through it. Your parents may not even have the strength to attend. You were loved, but you didn't care. Getting high with a bunch of kids was more important.

After your family settles in, a stream of extended family and friends will start rolling in. People they haven't seen in years will show up. They may do this just to say they were there and have something to talk about to their friends. Your drug use will be discussed behind your family's back, and they will be so proud their kids aren't using.

Your family will have to greet people and will break down and cry numerous times throughout the process. Someone may have made a collage of pictures of your life for people to look at as they stand in line. Your teachers, coaches, neighbors, co-workers, and friends of your extended family may come. Everyone who remembers you the way you were before you made that first bad choice will be there to support your family.

You will now have a ton of new friends who come to your funeral. Kids will show up who haven't spoken to you since kindergarten, but they will come so they also have something to talk about, "I went to _____'s funeral."

Your pre-drug friends will be there with tears in their eyes. They will talk about the fun you had together growing up. They will be sorry they didn't try harder to hang out with you when they saw you going down the wrong path. Why did you stop hanging with them? Did you think the drug friends were more fun? How much fun does getting high sound now?

Now for the best part of the funeral. The so called "friends" you got high with may or may not even show up. They are not your friends and they do not care about you. Getting high was all you had in common. A true friend would have tried to stop or help you. Most likely your drug friends blamed everything on you during the police investigation. It was all your idea. You went alone to buy the drugs, you started using first, and you convinced them to try different drugs. They will throw you under the bus and make up all types of stories to your parents and police portraying you as the one responsible for their problems. They will probably check themselves into rehab while you are the one who is dead. They will get a second chance, you didn't. Remember all the lies you told when you were using drugs?

Your drug pals are going to lie to everyone because that is what they are good at. If they are scared out of their minds because you died, they may give up enough information to lead police to the drug dealers. You will not be there to defend yourself.

They may have been there with you when you took your last drug and they probably ran away.

For the next few days or even weeks, your family will get visitors and cards. Then:

- The visitors stop coming.

- The calls become fewer and fewer.

- The cards stop coming.

- Your old friends have moved on and are back to doing what they did before you died.

Your family is now all alone to deal with the tragedy of your death because life has moved on for everyone else.

Other people can live, laugh, and go on normally. Your family will watch them and be envious. Your family is depressed with an indescribable sick painful feeling that comes and goes throughout the day for weeks and months to come. Every moment of each day during the first months will be a different emotion - anger, guilt, sorrow, depression. Often the pain of your death will be so intense they may hope they don't wake up in the morning so they won't have this horrible feeling one more day. Time can not pass fast enough for them. They want to feel better quickly, but it doesn't happen.

Everyone grieves in a different way. Each one of your family members will react differently. These differences can cause tension and fighting. They will have to suffer through this turmoil until each family member makes peace with what happened to you.

The reality that you are gone forever will start to sink in deeper each day. The ache and sadness only gets worse for them as the initial shock of your death wears off.

You have changed the path of your mother's, father's, brother's and sister's lives forever. A hole will be embedded in their hearts for the rest of their lives. You did this because you thought it was fun to try drugs.

Seven

LIFE WITHOUT YOU

You are dead. You are gone from this earth. There are no to-morrows for you. You will not see, touch or talk to your family ever again. They will not be able to see, touch or talk to **you** again. No one has any magical powers to bring you back. Your life is over.

You will never have any more birthdays.

You will never celebrate any holidays.

You will never be able to eat your favorite foods.

You will never be able to laugh at your favorite movies or shows.

You will never see your friends again.

You will not celebrate special moments with your family.

<u>You</u> will not have any special moments. No graduations, vacations, jobs, promotions, weddings, have children or become an aunt or uncle.

Whatever you have accomplished up to the age you die is **IT**. You probably didn't do much because you thought getting high was better than having life experiences. Close your eyes and think about this. You lost your life because of drugs. Think about what you will miss.

All that is left of you are memories.

At first, some of your family's memories of you may not be the greatest. You probably told each member of your family that they were "so annoying" or that you "hated them" so many times. They have been hurt by you before but this is a much different hurt. A hurt <u>they</u> know can kill you. You didn't care or try to help yourself because you continued to experiment.

While you were using drugs, you may have destroyed many of the relationships in your life.

- Your relationship with your parents.
- Your parent's relationship or marriage.
- Your relationships with your siblings.

You may have become violent, angry, or stolen from everyone. We all know you lied all the time. Regardless of what you did, you were still loved. Loved enough by your family for them to worry about you, care what you did when you went out, and try to talk to you about your life. Some of these family relationships will strengthen when you are dead, many can get worse. It is very common. Everyone will start to blame each other for what they did or did not do to help you. They will torment themselves for the rest of their lives thinking about what they could have done better to help you.

You know they did everything they could do, and it was you who didn't try hard enough. Getting high was more important. You let drugs and your friends control you.

All families are different. All parents are different. All mothers and fathers are not created equal. You may not have one or both of your parents in your life. You may not have felt loved evenly by both of them. You may not have any type of relationship with anyone in your family, but believe me you are loved by more people than you know. Don't wait until you are gone to see how many people care about you. Look at your family and think about how they try to show you they care.

Many young people think they are smarter than their parents. You may have had more of an education in different subjects and are more tech savvy than your parents, but they have had many more life experiences and have gained wisdom along the way. Because you can text faster does not mean you are smarter. Don't tune them out. Listen to what they say. They have been in situations where they had to make tough choices and hope that you, too, will make smart choices. The last thing they want is for you to become a statistic.

If you were lucky and your family knew about your drug use, they may have tried to help you by sending you to rehab or counseling. Whatever they did, while you were alive, there was **hope**:
- Hope you would stop using drugs.
- Hope you would stay strong and clean
- Hope you would have a long and happy life.

You blew it. The worst day of their lives is the day you die from drugs. Death is permanent and the hope is **gone**. What is left now is your family that is shattered, devastated and in the most incredible pain imaginable. As time goes on, better memories do come back, but the thought of your death is connected to each one. Every time your family members start to have a happy thought, the fact that you are dead creeps back into their minds. This brings the reality that you are gone forever right back to them. They will have emotional ups and downs. Initially after you die, the downs are more severe and frequent, but the ups will come slowly and in time.

Your death has caused your family to lose the capacity to enjoy anything 100% for the rest of their lives. They will enjoy again, but only partially.

You died because you were trying to fit in with a bunch of kids who most likely would have phased out of your life as time went on. Everyone goes on to different schools or jobs and makes new friends. Do you understand this? Truly think about what you are doing. Trying to fit in has killed you.

There are plenty of young people out there who do the same thing as you are doing **trying to fit in**. Look at whom you are trying to fit in with: kids who use drugs for fun and have no idea what they are snorting, smoking, injecting or swallowing. Kids who think nothing bad will ever happen to them. Kids who don't care about their futures, their bodies or their families.

Everyone wants friends and wants to belong to a group. You <u>can</u> have friends, and you can belong. Belong to a different type of group or your same group with different dynamics. One that doesn't need drugs to have fun. One that doesn't think getting wasted is the only way to have fun. You probably know many kids who don't want to start partying just to fit in. Stick with kids who feel the same way.

You may think trying drugs opens up a new world of friendships, but remember, these friendships are based on getting wasted. Your life is worth more than being friends with a bunch of kids who have made stupid choices that they definitely will regret some day. I promise you that!

Eight

YOUR MOTHER

Wow. I won't ever be able to find the words to describe what your death has done to the woman who raised you, loved you, protected you, and probably did everything humanly possible for you through your entire life. The woman you called "Mom." Not all moms are the same, but most moms love their children more than their own lives. We would do anything for our children.

Mothers who lose their children from drugs go through a slew of emotions every day. Guilt is probably the one that takes the longest to diminish. We feel guilty because our child used drugs and died. We feel as though we failed at our job of mothering. We feel guilty because we may have missed signs of drug use before it spiraled to an addiction and death. We feel guilty because we couldn't help our children overcome drug use. I feel guilty because I didn't know my son was using drugs and didn't get a chance to try to help him.

Your mother may ask herself every day, "'WHY? Why did my child experiment with dangerous drugs? What did I do wrong?

Where did we as a family go wrong? Why did my child make bad choices? Why do some kids die and others don't? Why?"

These are questions that will never be answered because you are gone and can't answer them. Your mother will have to try very hard not to torment herself for the rest of her life trying to figure out what she did wrong.

You willfully used drugs but somehow, your mother will blame herself for your drug use and your death.

Think about that the next time she gives you money, buys you a present, makes your favorite food, washes your clothes or gets you out of a jam.

Your mother will feel sadness that the child she loved and raised is gone forever. This is a feeling that will **never** go away. She will never see you again. She will never hear your voice. She will never hug you or kiss you. She will miss you every day.

Your mother will talk to you either through prayer, in her mind, or out loud as though you were sitting in the chair next to her. Your mother won't get to see you have wonderful life experiences or achieve the success she knew you were capable of before you started using drugs.

If you are in a single parent household, you have left your mother to suffer alone. Your siblings are grieving as well, but theirs is a different, but just as terrible, feeling. Your extended family will grieve, but it is not the same feeling as it is for your mother. Your mother will feel as though a part of her is missing every day for the rest of her life.

As she gets stronger, she may go for counseling or join a group of other mothers who lost kids because they thought it was fun to use drugs. She may join or start "Moms Against Drugs" groups. This won't work because as long as there are people buying drugs, the problem will never go away. She won't realize that fact, but fighting for you helps her. (We will discuss your drug dealer later.) Your mother may write a book to help her get stronger.

Remember, nothing will ever be the same for your entire family. Holidays, birthdays, and every occasion that your mother made special are now changed forever. She may go through the motions of life and will try to be there for the rest of the family, but your death has changed her and your family forever.

Part of your mother died when you did.

Nine

Your Father

Your death from drugs will destroy your father as much as your mother. Your dad will suffer silently and try to hold back his emotions to be strong for everyone. The man who taught you how to ride a bike, throw a ball, took you to the park and bought you ice cream is now shattered and broken.

A part of your father died when you did.

He will cry out loud or in his heart every day because you are dead. He will do it privately, maybe in the shower so the rest of the family doesn't see.

You were his son, his buddy.
His daughter, his little girl.

The child he bragged about to his friends. He was always so proud of you. Why did you change? Have you done anything to make your parents proud lately?

Not all fathers are created equal. If your father was not in your life, he probably will wish he had been. Your dad will feel incredibly guilty that he was not a good father.

Anger is tough for fathers to handle. Your dad will become angry at your drug friends and all of your friends. He will be angrier at your drug dealer. He will blame everyone in your world that you are dead and they are not.

The man who worked hard for money, for a home, food, clothes, and toys will blame himself for you going down the wrong path. He will blame himself if he <u>didn't</u> live with you. He will blame himself if he <u>did</u> live with you.

Your dad will wonder if things would have been different if only he hadn't worked so many hours, was around more, or if he worked more and made more money. Maybe he should have coached your team. Maybe he should have spent more time with you. Maybe he should have showed more interest in your hobbies. He will blame himself for everything that is wrong in your family.

After your death, the bills still have to be paid. Your dad will have to go back to work every day, and try not to break down in front of people. They will try to help him with clichés and quotes that are annoying. Your dad will refrain from telling them off because in his heart, he knows they are trying to help him.

Is getting high that much fun that you don't care whom you hurt? He would have helped you if you needed it. All you had to do was ask.

Ten

YOUR SIBLINGS

The only way to describe what your brothers and sisters will experience is for you to imagine how you would feel if **he or she** was the one who had died. If you don't have any siblings, think about a cousin or someone in your life you would consider as close to you as a brother or sister. You decided to mess with drugs and not only lost your life, but also you messed up the lives of your brothers and sisters as well.

When you die from drugs, your siblings will have lost someone who was their first, best, and sometimes only friend. The person they played with, fought with, teased, rough housed, hit, tickled, laughed with, sang with, slept with when scared and protected from harm. Holidays, birthdays, running, swimming, building snowmen. Think about how you played with your siblings when you were little. Brothers and sisters share the same childhood memories. They have a special bond.

For a long time, your siblings will live in denial that you are gone. They will pretend you are out with your friends or at school.

They will live in a false reality for many years to come. This may be the only way they can cope.

Every so often, they will experience reality checks; **YOU ARE GONE**. Every happy moment in the rest of their lives will be tainted with a feeling of sadness that you are not there to share it. They will force themselves to try to embrace joyous occasions for a long time to come.

A part of your brother and sister died when you did.

They lost the best man or maid of honor at their wedding. Their children lost an aunt or uncle and they will not have any cousins. Your siblings will have to explain to their own children someday that they used to have a brother or sister who died from using drugs. Is that the legacy you want to leave for your family; being the aunt or uncle who died from drugs?

Your older siblings will wish it was them who died instead of you. You didn't get a chance to experience life. They will feel guilty. They will be angry at first, but the anger subsides and the pain becomes deeper. If they had to fill in for your parents during the funeral planning, they will have a delayed reaction to your death. Believe me, it will come soon. The anger, guilt, and depression will hit them like a bat. Every aspect of their lives will be affected for a very long time.

They will wonder why you did this. Why did you fool around with drugs you knew could kill you? Why didn't you listen to them? They would have helped you if you asked. Why didn't your friends go to them and tell them what you were doing?

Your siblings' significant others will be just as affected and experience the same tremendous pain and grief. If they were around for a long time and watched you grow up, they will have also lost a brother or sister. They will have to be there for your family through their grief and they may have to be the strong ones.

A part of them died when you did as well.

Your younger siblings will wonder why you left them. Why aren't you there to help them through life? Your death has taken away part of their youth. You forced them to grow up fast, and take on roles they were not ready to handle.

You are not there to watch over them. They may try to do what you did, experiment with drugs that can kill them. Would you like your little sister to use drugs? How would you feel if she snorts some coke or injects some heroin? How about if she hooks up with some drug dealer to get drugs? How about your little brother? Imagine him getting high at a party? Picture him getting wasted and acting reckless. How about if he takes some Molly that is laced with some type of poison? Scary isn't it?

Your siblings will be the kids at school whose brother or sister died from drugs. They will be stared at, talked about, and they will lose many of their friends. Young people are not equipped to deal with a grieving friend, so your brother or sister will be avoided and left alone to deal with your death.

Very young siblings may experience a bias from their friends' parents. The parents may not want your sibling in their house because he or she is associated with someone who used or uses drugs. They may treat your family members as though they have a contagious disease.

Things will never be the same in your house. This scenario could go in many different directions. You know how your family functions behind closed doors. Think about what you will do to your little sister or little brother if you die from drugs.

You have left emptiness in the hearts of your brothers and sisters that will never be filled. If you have more than one sibling, they will have each other to lean on. Your death may make them closer or it could push them apart. If you only have one, you have left him or her alone to deal with your death and to be the strong one for your family.

The next time you think about getting high, make sure you say something nice to them before you leave the house. That may be the last time you ever talk to them. In fact, you should say something nice to everyone before you go out. You don't want them to remember you calling each other names, text fighting or cursing at each other as their last contact with you. The last text you send to each member of your family will be the memory of their last contact with you.

The last words you say to them will be what they will remember forever.

Eleven

Your Significant Other

You have died and left your girlfriend or boyfriend. He or she has lost the love of his or her young life. Your loved one has lost the hopes and dreams for the two of you together.

If this person was the one to find you dead, either alone or along with your family, he or she will have this vision of you every day for a long time. Other symptoms your significant other may experience: problems sleeping, eating, or functioning for an unending time period. He or she will possibly need professional help along with medication.

Your romantic partner will start to feel alone and that no one understands his or her pain: not parents, friends, or coworkers. In the beginning, he or she may stay with your family more because they all feel the same bond, your death.

Your girlfriend or boyfriend will become angrier and angrier at you for using drugs. Initially, the person will feel betrayed, especially after learning how much you lied to everyone. Then he or she will feel guilty, especially if this person didn't try to get you help. He or she will have difficulty accepting that you are gone and will pretend you are sleeping.

Unless you lose a relative, it is expected that you return to school or work within a week after a funeral. Your girlfriend or boyfriend will be forced to try to get back to "normal" quicker than the ability to cope dictates. No one will understand there is a new normal going on, one that people outside your circle can't possibly understand.

Initially, your boyfriend or girlfriend will become the most popular person in school or at work. Everybody will want to be a friend. That wears off as quickly for this person as it did for your family. Your special person will be stared at, talked about, and known as the person whose boyfriend or girlfriend died from drugs.

Your boyfriend or girlfriend has now learned firsthand the seriousness of what can happen when kids experiment with drugs. Most kids didn't learn a thing from your death and will not want anyone around to ruin the party. Your boyfriend or girlfriend will need to find new friends because invitations to hang out will stop coming. He or she will have trouble dating and may wonder if love will ever come again.

Think about what you would do if the person you are in love with dies. How would you feel?

Twelve

THE DRUG DEALER

*H*ere is some news about the person you buy drugs from:

1. Your drug dealer does not care about you or your good time.

2. Your drug dealer is not your friend. Even if you buy from someone you know from school or your town, this person is not your friend.

3. Your drug dealer will sell drugs to a 10 year old to make money. That could be your little brother or sister. This drug dealer may use his little brother or sister or his <u>own children</u> to sell drugs.

4. Your drug dealer wants you addicted to ensure a steady stream of customers.

5. As long as there are customers, there will be drug dealers. (Remember the laws of supply and demand.)

6. You do not know where the drugs come from. The supply of chemicals used in the drugs is manufactured all over the world. There is no oversight to make sure the product is of any particular quality.

You do not know what you are smoking, snorting, swallowing or injecting.

7. You may think you are buying one type of drug but it could be full of all types of fillers like medications used for animals or anesthetics. You may not find out until it is too late. Your family will find out for you if you die.

8. Your drug dealer is not a chemist or pharmacist although he may think he is. This person does not know how to prepare doses consistently or accurately nor does he care if he does. Each batch of drugs is prepared in drug mills and each batch differently.

Drug dealers use unskilled, untrained people to prepare and package your drugs in dirty, filthy conditions.

9. Your drug dealer uses all types of substances in the drugs just to increase profit; crap that will poison you and can kill you.

10. If caught by the police, your drug dealer will rat out his customers. If this person uses any type of phone app, it can be traced.

Police will be calling you in for questioning.

11. Your drug dealer will hurt you or kill you if he needs to.

- Drug dealers want to make money.

- They do not want to work hard.

- They want easy money so they sell drugs to kids.

- All they care about is the money. END OF STORY!

You lost your life and destroyed your family while making some lazy, sleazy, dirt bag, lowlife drug dealer rich.

Thirteen

OVERDOSING

Here are some facts for you to think about if you overdose:

You may live but you do not know what effects your overdose will have on your brain or your body. For example:

1. You can have irreversible brain damage from lack of oxygen.

Your brain being deprived of oxygen can cause the following:

    a. You can wind up in a coma on life support.
    b. You will live in a nursing home until you die:

- You will wear diapers.

- You can get bed sores from not moving.

- You will need to have your saliva and mucous suctioned out of your mouth with a machine.

- Your hands, arms, legs and feet can become contracted and curled up.

- You will need a feeding tube.

- Someone may have to make a decision to take you off life support and you will die sooner.

2. Depending on the part of your brain that is damaged and the extent of the damage, this is what could happen to you:

a. You will not think or understand anything the way you used to. You will never be able to drive a car.

b. You may need extensive rehabilitation with cognitive, physical, occupational and speech therapy. This is different from substance abuse rehab.

c. You can become blind or suffer from vision problems. This could be permanent.

d. You may never walk again. You may need a wheelchair to get around for the rest of your life.

e. You may not be able to use your arms and hands or your legs and feet. You will need braces and splints.

f. Someone may have to push your wheelchair around because you can't do it yourself.

g. Even if you are not in a coma, you could wind up wearing diapers. You may not be able to get on and off a toilet. You will need someone else to wipe your butt for the rest of your life.

h. You may never talk again. You may drool. You may make weird noises.

i. If you can still chew and swallow, someone will still have to feed you.

j. Or, you may need a feeding tube and will be fed only liquids.

k. You may need a cane to walk. You may not be able to go up and down stairs. You will shake when you try to use the side of your body most affected.

l. You may need someone to pick you up and transfer you in and out of a chair or your bed.

m. You will need someone else to give you a shower and wash your hair.

n. You will never be able to live alone. You will need someone to be with you around the clock.

o. You may need someone else to do <u>everything</u> for you.

p. You may need to have expensive changes made to your home for you to be able to live there while in a wheelchair. Your home will need ramps, widened doorways, special showers, staircase chairlifts or an elevator.

q. If your family can't take care of you at home or afford the home modifications, you will have to live in a facility if they can find one that can accommodate you.

r. You can have one, two or all of these problems from overdosing.

Watch how fast your friends dump you! They may visit for a few months, but they will go on with their lives and forget about you. I see this happen every day.

This is just a snap shot of what brain damage can do to you. Your heart, lungs, kidneys, liver, all your organs and your bowels and bladder function can become affected as well. Go online and look up anoxic brain injury, organ failure, and the complications of immobility if you don't believe me. Your family may not be able to take care of you. They may not have the money to pay for help. You have now put them in a different type of living hell.

Sounds like fun doesn't it? Diapers and needing someone else to feed you, bathe you, cook for you, make decisions for you and to wipe your butt is not fun. Is getting high worth it?

Really, pay attention.

Think about what you are doing.

Stop experimenting before it's too late.

Nothing good will ever come of drug use.

Find something else to do with your free time. It's not worth it.

If you are addicted, **get help** and do what it takes to stay strong. You have to want to be helped. You don't want to die or end up brain damaged.

Fourteen

THE NEXT PARTY

*O*k, now you know the reality of death from drugs and overdosing. Many of these chapters can apply if you drink too much as well so don't think this only happens when you experiment with drugs. I asked you to think about this in the beginning of this book. Go back to that first time you agreed to try some type of substance. Was it worth it?

Think about this book the next time you are out with your friends or at a party: kids are high on whatever drug they choose, kids are doing shots or guzzling beer like its soda. Think about what can happen to you. It is time for you to make some tough choices.

Are you going to cave and do what they are doing, or are you going to look at them, realize they are acting like assholes and get out?

Somewhere over the years, things have changed. Kids think the only way to have fun is to get wasted. It is a different world out there now than it was a few years ago. Experimenting can kill you. Trying to fit in by partying can kill you.

Think about the chapter of this book that had the most impact on you. Maybe you should read it before you go out!

No one is telling you not to have fun with your friends. No one is telling you not to socialize and go to parties. Socializing is fun when you act smart, and don't attempt to fit in by doing something that is risky. Someone is always the one who tries the drugs and drinking first and others follow. Don't be the one to start, don't be the one to encourage others, and don't be the one who follows.

The information in this book is real. It is what happens to you and your family. This is not information you get in school or drug awareness classes. It should be. Maybe we would have less addicts and deaths. This book contains details you need to know when you are faced with choices and before you make a very big mistake. Are you going to try to fit in with the idiots who think it is fun, or are you going to say no?

You have the power to make the choice. You can have fun without drugs or alcohol. If you can't, you have a problem. GET HELP!!!

Now, after reading all the horrible things that can happen to you and your family from experimenting with drugs, do you think getting high is worth it? Look at what your decision to try drugs has done:

You lost your life
You devastated your family
You helped a drug dealer get rich

It's time for the choice. Are you going to become a statistic? Or, will you decide not to risk your life?

Fifteen

A Personal Statement

7 Years Later

The message below was written by a sister.   Seven years later, her family is still devastated. This can be your family at any time if you continue to get involved with drugs.

Seven years ago, I was a different person. I was genuinely happy, my smile was real, and my family was put together. Today I live in denial with a false smile and a fake world. I pretend you're alive; out with your friends, snowboarding, cruising in your car. Your room and bathroom are perfectly intact. I enforce it. I make sure everything stays as is. It has to because otherwise I'd realize you aren't here. I have become obsessive over your belongings. Your toothpaste still sits how you left it on the counter and your dirty laundry is still in your hamper. It's an illness and an obsession. I have to keep it that way to enforce the fact that I'm not alone. I'm sick.

Then there are the reality checks. You're not here. Mom and Dad are fighting – again. It's bad. It's really bad. They are getting a divorce. They still throw your name into it. I know if you were here it wouldn't be this bad. There I stand; alone and isolated. Where are you? You told me you weren't going to leave me. I have no one to talk to or confide in. How could you do this to us? How could you do this to me? I need you. You destroyed our family.

Some days I don't think I'm going to make it. I'm sure people can see through my fake happiness, but I push forward for Mom's sake. You should see her. It is like she aged 15 years. She's really good at playing pretend and putting on a front, but when she doesn't know anyone is listening – it's heart aching. She still yells out to you. Can you hear her? Can you hear how devastated she is? Imagine how this makes me feel. Dad cries in the shower. EVERY SHOWER. My bedroom is on the opposing side of his bathroom. He doesn't realize I can hear everything. How am I supposed to push forward and be well when you have killed our parents? Our home is no longer a home; it is a living hell house.

Sometimes I pretend to be you. I'll hear a song on the radio that I know you would like. I blast it and yell out to you. I often wonder if you can hear me. Other times I scream like a maniac. I have to. I need to let it out. If I don't let it out, I get sick. I do this at least once a month. Mind you – it's been over seven years since you've been gone.

I graduated college two years after you left. I didn't walk at the graduation ceremony. I graduated with a master's degree five years after you left. I didn't walk at the graduation ceremony. I refused to have a graduation party. I got into dental school six years after you left. I didn't have a celebratory party. Why? It's too much of a reality check. I can't do it. Even after numerous years, I'm still not strong enough. I have deprived myself from honorable and positive experiences because I know you won't be there.

Do you know what that has done to me? I'm shattered. Even after all these years, I'm still emotionally damaged. You ruined me. You took away my happiness. You took away the joys that I should have been able to experience like everyone else my age. It's so unfair.

Christmas morning used to be my favorite day of the year – hands down. The smell of Mom's French toast, the fireplace going, laughter filling the air, and an abundance of presents! Holidays have now gone from one extreme to another. I despise Christmas morning. It terrifies me. How am I expected to wake up and open presents without you? You should see us now; it's pathetic. We have no spirit – there's no Christmas tree decorating or music playing. So thanks a lot for taking that away from me, too.

You decided to mess with drugs. You decided to destroy your life. So why is it that you ended up destroying mine? I don't understand. You ruined me. I deserved to have a happy adolescence. I deserved to enjoy my twenties. Why did you take that from me? I'll never be an Aunt and you'll never be an Uncle. That's devastating. So congratulations, you have officially ruined all the moments that are supposed to bring me happiness.

The hurt and the pain have only gotten worse with each passing year. The more I begin to realize that you are not coming home, the more my heart feels like it is being ripped out of my chest. I hate that you did this to me, I hate that I have to face the world by myself, and I hate that you couldn't just get clean.

So here I stand with my fake smile pretending you are alive and well. I live one day at a time because if I think about tomorrow, I won't get through today. I'll always love you and you'll always be my big bro – but you sure made a mess of things. I hope it was worth it.

Sixteen

How To Ask for Help

It is never too late or too early to ask for help. Don't be afraid, just understand your family will be upset at first, but they love you <u>unconditionally</u> and will do anything they can to help you. Your family does not want you to die. Recognizing you need help is the first step toward becoming drug free. Remember what you read in this book. Getting high can kill you.

Do not tell your family in a public place. Do it at home so the truth and all the emotions that will follow can be expressed freely.

If you have difficulty finding the words to tell your family, remember to always start with an apology:

"I am sorry this happened, I didn't mean to get out of control. I didn't really understand the dangers of drugs. I would never want to hurt you".

"Mom, Dad I need help." Tell them exactly what you have been doing, what you are taking, and how often you are using.

You will feel better telling the truth and no longer having to live a lie. If you stole anything from them, now is the time to come clean about everything.

Be prepared to take whatever comes out from your family. Sit and be quiet, it will be over eventually and they can then process what you told them. Answer all their questions and tell the truth! No one starts out wanting to become an addict; it can happen to anyone at anytime. If your parents do not know about drugs, they will have to learn this very quickly. Give them time to learn and understand what has happened to you. They will then work on helping you. Remember it is a shock for them if they did not know what you were doing. It will be a relief for them if they did know and can now work with you to get you clean. They love you more than you will ever understand, even if they yell and scream, take everything away from you or punish you. It is because they love you.

Don't argue about any restrictions placed on you. It is for your own good. You will recognize this some day.

If you cannot get the words out of your mouth, you can write a letter to them. Remember to tell the absolute truth.

You can ask someone to be with you when you tell them or when they read the letter. Whatever it takes to get help, do!

If you are unsure if you need help, answer one question; do you need drugs or alcohol to have a good time? If the answer is yes, you have a problem or are on the way toward one. Get help before it is too late.

Helping a Friend

If you have a friend whose drug use is out of control, please let your friend's family know. Addiction is complicated and your friend will probably need professional help. Do not try to intervene on your own. You may mean well, but you may do more harm than good trying to help someone who may be out of control.

Ask your parents or an adult you trust for the best way to approach your friend's family. Perhaps your mothers are friends and having your mother take the lead on this would be best. Is there a favorite teacher you could trust to follow up? If all else fails, think about writing a letter to your friend's parents. As difficult as that may seem, you do not want to experience the guilt and pain that follows if your friend dies from drugs and you did not try to get help.

If your friend or his or her family gets mad at you for telling, don't worry. You have done the right thing. Someday, they will thank you.

Seventeen

MORE MESSAGES

- Nothing good will come from experimenting with drugs.

- Find other ways to have fun.

- Don't try so hard to fit in with kids who want to grow up fast and want to be wild. There are plenty of kids out there who feel just like you. Stick together and you can have fun without getting wasted.

- Your parents work hard for their money. You may work hard for your money also. Using hard earned money to buy drugs hurts your family and makes a disgusting drug dealer rich.

- Only you have the power to help yourself.

- Don't sign yourself out of rehab if you are of age. Finish the program and work on getting better.

- Go to counseling, pray, do whatever it takes to show you are stronger than drugs.

- If you know your friends are using drugs and making bad choices, tell someone so they get help. You only lose a friend when they are gone forever. Don't let them die. They will thank you some day.

- Choose to live a long happy life. The choices you make now will affect you for the rest of your life.

- Do not be afraid to ask your family for help. Of course they will be upset when they find out but believe me, they will help you. If you are fearful of telling them, ask a sibling, an aunt or uncle, a teacher, clergy or someone you trust to be with you when you speak to them.

You don't want to die and your family does not want to lose you.

In loving memory

of

Daniel Marcel Lajterman

August 9, 1994 – February 23, 2014

We love you always and miss you every day.

Mom, Dad, Michael, Andrea and Alex and Colleen

If tears could build a stairway,
And memories a lane, I'd walk right up to Heaven
And bring you home again.
(Author Unknown)

Made in the USA
Charleston, SC
05 April 2016